CW00401631

To...........................

From.........................

Purple Ronnie's

Reasons Why You're a

SUPER MUM

LOVE YOU

by Purple Ronnie

First published 2010 by Boxtree
an imprint of Pan Macmillan, a division of Macmillan Publishers Limited
Pan Macmillan, 20 New Wharf Road, London N1 9RR
Basingstoke and Oxford
Associated companies throughout the world
www.panmacmillan.com

ISBN 978-0-7522-2720-7

Copyright © 2003, 2010 Purple Enterprises Ltd, a Coolabi company

Some of the material in this book was previously published as Purple Ronnie's Little Thoughts About Mums

All rights reserved. No part of this publication may be
reproduced, stored in or introduced into a retrieval system, or
transmitted, in any form, or by any means (electronic, mechanical,
photocopying, recording or otherwise) without the prior written
permission of the publisher. Any person who does any unauthorized
act in relation to this publication may be liable to criminal
prosecution and civil claims for damages.

9 8 7 6 5 4 3 2 1

A CIP catalogue record for this book is available from the British Library.

Printed and bound in Hong Kong

'Purple Ronnie' created by Giles Andreae. The right of Giles Andreae and Janet Cronin
to be identified respectively as the author and illustrator of this work has been asserted by them
in accordance with the Copyright, Designs and Patents Act 1988.

Visit **www.panmacmillan.com** to read more about all our books
and to buy them. You will also find features, author interviews and
news of any author events, and you can sign up for e-newsletters
so that you're always first to hear about our new releases.

a poem about a

Super Mum

You cook, you clean, you
tidy
You're a five star taxi too
So here's a massive thank
you
To a mum as great as you!

a poem about a

Top Mum

If someone was giving out
medals
To say what a top mum you
are
You would be told
You'd be getting the gold
Cos you are the greatest by
far!

Sometimes even your mum needs looking after.
Be there when she needs you.

frazzled mum
I'm so tired
don't worry Mum. I'll make you a cup of tea

a poem about

My Mummy

You're such a special mummy

And I love the things you do

So I want to say you're lovely

And thanks for being <u>YOU</u>!

a poem about

Mummy Love

When I was a little child
And frightened in the
night

You knew just how to
comfort me
And make me feel alright

there, there dear, it was just a dream
the...the... monster... he... chased me!
rock
my angel

Waking Up

Who needs an alarm clock when you've got a Mum?

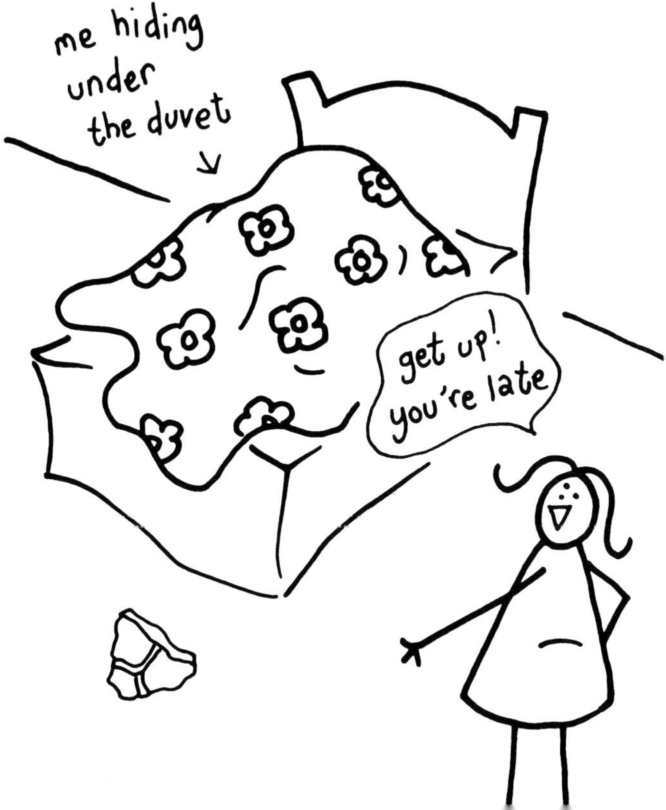
me hiding under the duvet
get up! you're late

a poem for a

Wonderful Mum

You give advice, you help me
out

And show me that you care

So thanks for being brilliant

And for always being there!

a poem for a

Special Mum

You're a very special person
And you mean a lot to me
When you're around
You make the world
A better place to be

Some Mums never stop thinking that you're still their little baby

a poem about a

Fab Mum

Sometimes as mums become
older

Their bodies start showing the
weather

Their things start to droop and
to dangle

But you look more gorgeous
than ever!

dazzle

a poem about my

Mum's Cooking

I've dined in fancy restaurants
And swanky bistros too
But I've yet to find a
          gastro-chef
Who cooks as well as you!

here you go dear
beam
mum's amazing roast dinner
drool
... mmm
gravy

All mums need a hobby. Some mums really love their garden

a poem about

Mums

Some mums are pretty amazing
Cos no matter how busy they
seem
They always are there for
their family
That crazy but wonderful
team!

a poem for an

Amazing Mum

Mums are just totally brilliant

They cook and they wash and
they clean

So here is a poem that's just
to say thanks

To the world's greatest
multi-task queen!

All mums deserve
a treat from time
to time

My Mum's an Angel

I think my mum's an angel
She does so many things
But if She IS an angel
Where DOES she keep
her wings?

a poem for a

Groovy Mum

You're supercool and gorgeous

You're as lovely as can be

And guess what mum - the best thing is

You've passed it all to me!

us being
supercool

Mums like to be remembered on their birthdays. It's mostly the thought that counts

I made it myself!
soaked in orange squash
MUM
bits of mud
it's lovely dear

a poem about an

Ace Mum

This poem is simply to tell you
The reason why you are so
great
You're not only brilliant at
being a mum
You're also a really top mate!

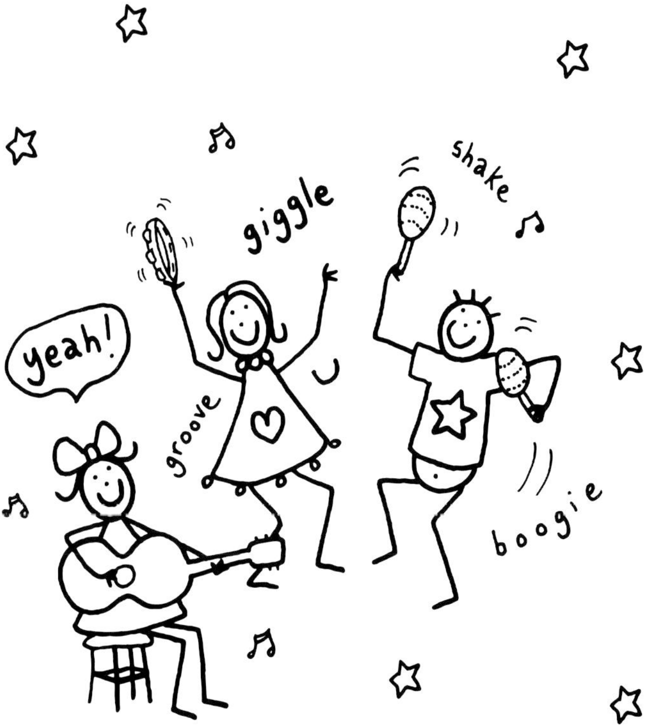

yeah!
giggle
shake
groove
boogie

Mum

I love you cos you're caring
And you're kind and thoughtful
too
But most of all I love you,
mum
Because, well...you are YOU!

Mums can often give good advice on all sorts of things

dream girl
if you want her to notice you, what you have to do is go and say hello
uh?

a poem about a

Top Mum Prize

You can't be young forever,
mum

But the wrinkles round your
eyes

Were earned with all the
love you gave

So you get Top Mum's Prize!

a poem about

Fab Cake

I wonder what your secret
is

When you get down to bake,

Because it's true that only
you

Can make a mum-type cake

mum's
perfect
sponge
cake

my
flat
disaster

top
secret
recipe

Some mums are happier going out to work

a poem about

Mums Being in Charge

Mums have voices sweet and soft

Until they flip, and boom:

"Don't you talk to me like that!

Go up to your room!"

a poem about a

Great Mum

Thanks for everything you are
And all the things you've
done
You know it's true
You really are
The world's most brilliant
mum!

a poem for

My Nº1 Mum

Some mums may be famous,
But rest assured, you're fine
No matter what you may
achieve
The main thing is: You're MINE!

a poem about

Mum Talk

Mums are good at comforting
And being extra nice,
But sometimes Mums know better
And dish out stern advice!

EXAMPLE A

EXAMPLE B

a poem about

My Special Mum

We only get one mum
supplied
We can't go out and buy one
Thank goodness then that
I got you
So that, of all, you're MY ONE!

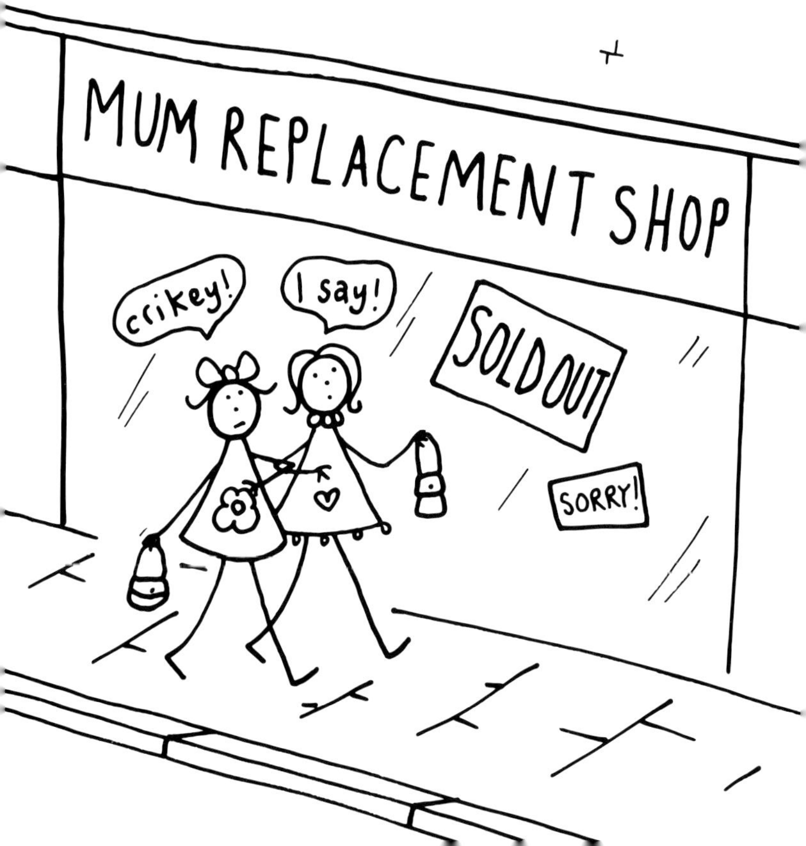
MUM REPLACEMENT SHOP
crikey!
I say!
SOLD OUT
SORRY!

a poem about being

My Smashing Mum

The world is full of people

And I take them as they
come

But out of all those millions–

You're my only Mum!

you are
amazing

↓

Thank You